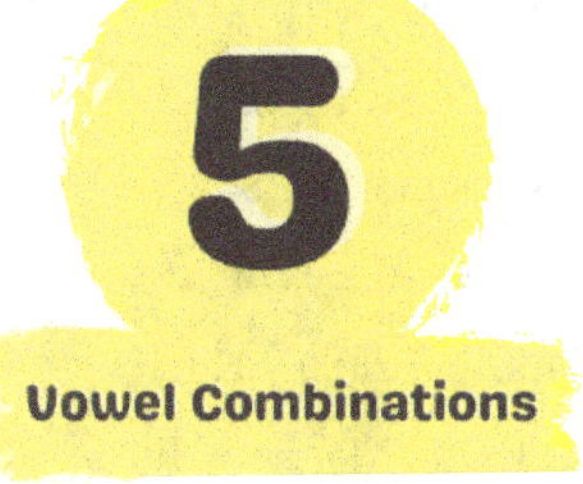

PRESCHOOL PHONICS

WARNING!

Lots of crazy words!

i

Author: Matthew Hitch

Co-author: Sunok Moon

Illustrator: Matthew Hitch

Cover Design: Brittany Hitch

Layout Design: Matthew Hitch

Text Design: Matthew Hitch

Image Manager: Matthew Hitch

~~Vain Meglomaniac: Matthew Hitch~~

Credits Editor: Matthew Hitch

Image Manager Manager: S. Moon

Image Manager Manager Control: Absolutely no one

Artistic Arguer: Sunok Moon

Dishwasher: Matthew Hitch (occasionally Sunok Moon)

Title: Captain Matt's Super Crazy Fun Preschool Phonics 5 Student Book

ISBN 979-11-982546-9-6

First published 2023

Published by Hitch Publishing

info@supercrazyfun.net

This textbook came about as the result of 20 years of trying to make kids enjoy learning English. It is designed around the use of the rhotic R and other characteristics of English pronunciation common in North America. We believe it can be used in other parts of the world as most phonics books can, and we are keen to hear feedback from anyone who tries this.

We want to make clear that the word "crazy" used in the title is in relation to any of the common definitions illustrated below, and does not refer in any way to the meaning "insane."

strange/illogical   **wild**   **unexpected**   **fun**   **unwise**

About the Authors:

Matthew Hitch has taught English in Korea for the better part of 20 years and holds a master's degree in applied linguistics. He clearly does not have a pig nose, and by most accounts is not at all malodorous. He also cuts a dashing figure according to his wife.

Sunok Moon prefers to go by the name Michelle, and is in fact quite scary as reported in the bio on the back of this book. She has a degree in English literature and has taught English in Korea for approximately 3 weeks longer than Matthew, who is writing this and finds it weird to refer to himself in the third person.

Contents

Welcome parents and teachers!

Thank you for considering our book. Phonics books are notoriously boring, so this is the last bastion of publishing where even the tiniest bit of creativity can raise the bar (sorry phonics book publishers, but it's true). With that said, we humbly offer you our content. We have also intentionally challenged convention in a few ways. Much of what we have to say may be used or discarded though, and these books can be used just like any other mainstream phonics book. We hope you will choose to use whatever you please and dispose of the rest.

Please allow us to explain just where our method of teaching phonics may diverge from mainstream approaches, and please do forgive us for sharing information from what is undeniably the most mind-numbingly boring and seemingly useless field of study, linguistics. Most phonics books are not written by scholars in the field of linguistics. They are mostly written by early childhood educators, so perhaps that's the first divergence. We'll start with how we sound out consonants. In linguistic studies it is not uncommon for consonants to be distinguished by using a vowel (usually "ah") on both sides. This means a "V" sounds like "ahvah" and an "F" sounds like "ahfah" and so on. Most phonics books distinguish consonant sounds without such preceding vowel, but they do follow with a vowel in the form of the schwa. This is fine for most consonants, but the ones that are able to be maintained until breath is exhausted can be confusing with a schwa where they end a word. It's mostly ESL students who feel this confusion, but we think it doesn't hurt to teach those consonants without a schwa to native speakers as well, so where "V" sounds like "və" in most phonics books, in our book it is presented as "vvvvvvv" with no schwa. We apply this to all long consonant sounds in our audio files (L,M,N&R are also presented as long with a tiny schwa sound at the end though). If you have read this far, we take our hats off to you. Most would be fast asleep by now.

The next divergence is our use of Magic E. We chose Magic E for the fun
potential. The Split Digraphs just can't seem to hold a crowd. Magic E is no
longer used in most educational settings for many reasons, but mostly because
as a rule it cannot be defined clearly. We do mention that split digraphs are
better though, mainly to extend an olive branch to all the teachers we hope
will buy our books.

And the final divergence we would like to mention is our choice of words. Our
choice of words may seem a bit odd at times throughout the books, but we
chose them for their potential for keeping kids engaged over their usefulness.
We approach a phonics book as a tool to teach about sounds much more
than vocabulary. Poop, vomit, spit, fart, snot, and burp are the most popular
with our students. We tried to find a spot for booger, but alas...

Our word choice is also strange in that it includes words that have the long
E vowel when teaching split digraphs. Most phonics books glance over the
long E vowel. The argument we have heard for this is that it is difficult for
the younger students, but we suspect that it's avoided more because it's
difficult for authors to find suitable words. We decided to give it a try, and
our experience is that the long E words we chose are not that difficult for our
students to grasp. Given that English is their second language, we believe
native English speaking kids will cope with them just fine. Also you may notice
our sight words are not all actually sight words - oops! Anyway, we hope you
enjoy our silly books.

Welcome students!

Tracks 0-9

Now we will learn how to put letters together to make new vowel sounds. Sometimes we put vowel letters together, and sometimes vowel and consonant letters together. Making these new vowel sounds can be difficult.

We have to memorize lots of different sounds for many of the same pairs of letters. Sometimes it might feel impossible, but we can do it!

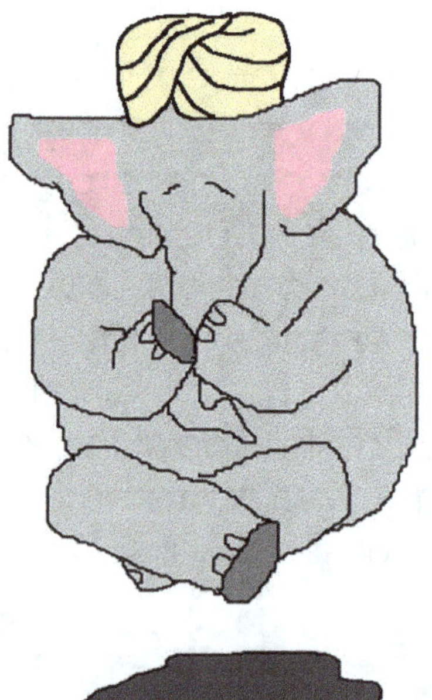

We have to memorize them
because they don't make their
usual sounds.
Sometimes it seems even THEY
don't know what they're doing.

We can't control them. Our job is just
to learn all the new sounds they make
together.

Let's get started...

Vowels

Let's practice them before we start.

 Tracks 0-9

Name	short sound	
A	a	😃
E	e	😄
I	i	😐
O	o	😮
U	u	😐

i and u can be VERY short!

Remember the consonant blends? Vowels also go together like that, but they don't blend quite as well as consonants. They usually make a whole new sound.

Vowel Combinations

When vowels get together to make a new vowel sound they change and swap their sounds. It's very confusing. We have to use our memory a lot.

The funny thing about these new vowel sounds is that consonants can join in too! They all change their sounds like there are no rules, but there is one rule. Vowels are on the left and consonants are on the right!

UNIT 1   Vowel Combinations

Listen, point, and make the sound:  

Words with *ai, ay, ee, ea*

1 **ai** **ay**

2 **ea** **ee**

Listen, point, and say the word: 

1 w + **ai**t = w**ai**t  wait

2 tr + **ee** = tr**ee**  tree

3 d + **ay** = d**ay**  day

Follow the rules

Write the words

1 ea + t = ___________ 

2 s + ail = ___________ 

3 t + eeth = ___________

4 pl + ay = ___________ 

New Words

Listen, point and repeat the new words

Track 9

ai

| sail | train | wait |

ay

| day | play | say |

ee

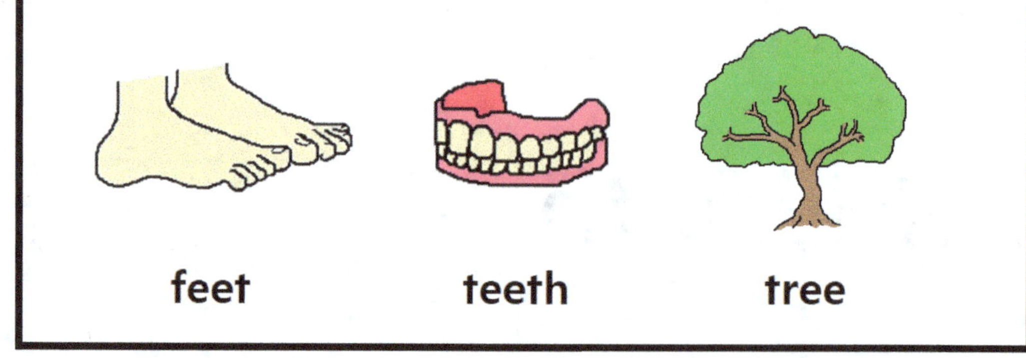

| feet | teeth | tree |

ea

| eat | meat | teach |

Exercises

Listen and complete the word

Track **10**

Tracks 10-19

1 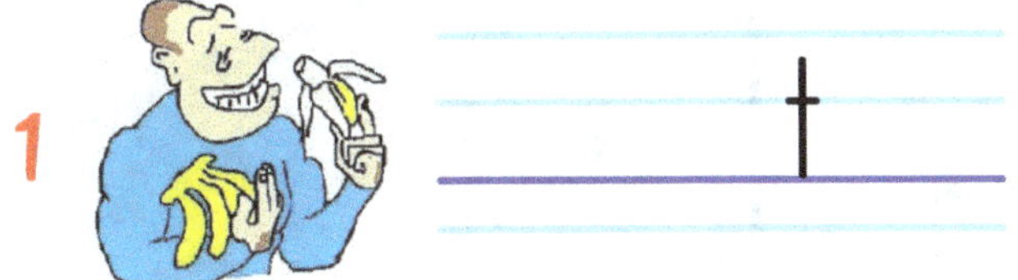 _ _ t

2  m _ t

3 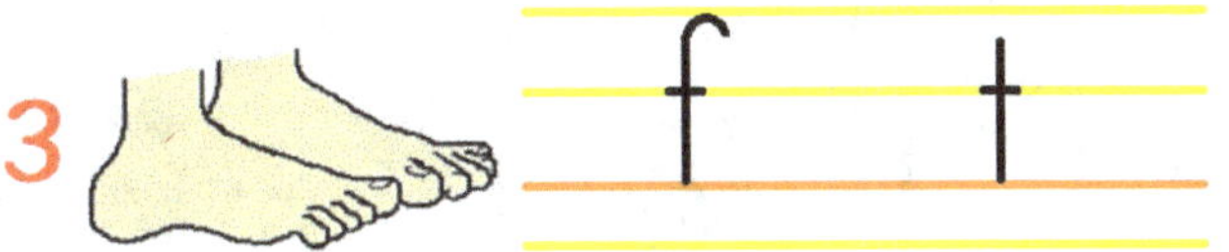 f _ t

4  s _ _

5  w _ t

6  d _ _

Listen and circle the right letters AND picture

Track **11**

1 ai ee ay ea 

2 ai ee ay ea 

3 ai ee ay ea 

4 ai ee ay ea  

5 ai ee ay ea 

6 ai ee ay ea  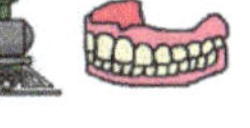

Exercises

Circle the word you hear

Circle the vowel sound you hear

1. ai ee ay ea   2. ai ee ay ea

3. ai ee ay ea   4. ai ee ay ea

Chant

New sight words: with way

I eat meat
With my feet

People say
Don't eat that way!

But I eat meat
With my feet

I do it every day!

12   Unit 1

Story

Write the word to match the picture

Tracks 10-19

1 

2 

3 

4 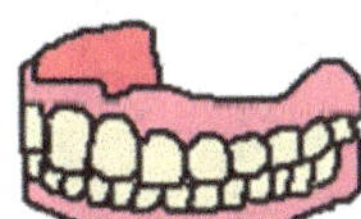

Listen and read along

Track 15

New sight words: please or

UNIT 2   Vowel Combinations

Listen, point, and make the sound:   Track 16   Words with oa, ow, oi, oy

Tracks 10-19

1   **oa ow**

2   **oi oy**

Listen, point, and say the word:  Track 17

1 b + oat = boat    boat

2 b + oil = boil   boil

3 b + owl = bowl   bowl

Follow the rules

Write the words

1 b + oy = __________

2 c + oat = __________

3 t + oilet = __________

4 sl + ow = __________

New Words

Tracks 10-19

Listen, point and repeat the new words

oa

| boat | coat | soap |

ow

| bowl | slow | throw |

oi

| boil | noise | toilet |

oy

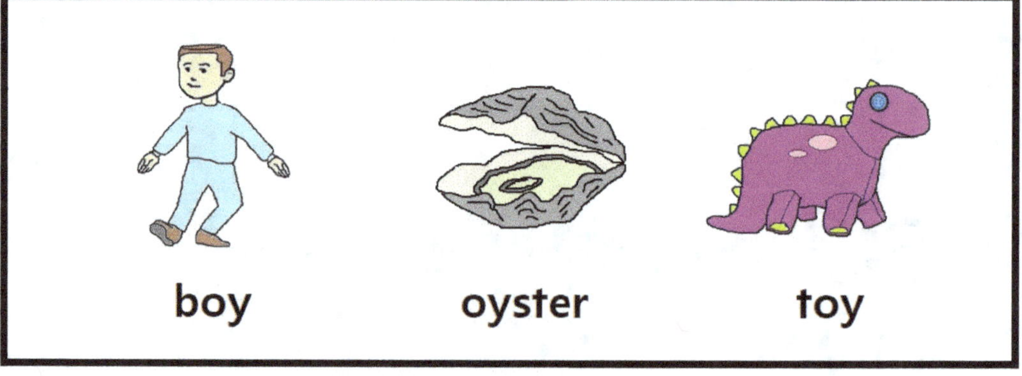

| boy | oyster | toy |

Exercises

Listen and complete the word

1  t_ let

2  __ster

3  b

4  s__p

5  c__t

6  thr__

Listen and circle the right letters AND picture

1 oa oi ow oy 

2 oa oi ow oy 

3 oa oi ow oy 

4 oa oi ow oy 

5 oa oi ow oy 

6 oa oi ow oy 

Exercises

Circle the word you hear

Tracks 20-29

Track 21

Circle the vowel sound you hear

Track 22

1. oa oi ow oy   2. oa oi ow oy

3. oa oi ow oy   4. oa oi ow oy

Chant

Track 23

New sight words: them

Boil oysters in a toilet

Put soap in.

Boil oysters in a toilet

Throw them in the bin!

18   Unit 2

Story

Write the word to match the picture

1 

2 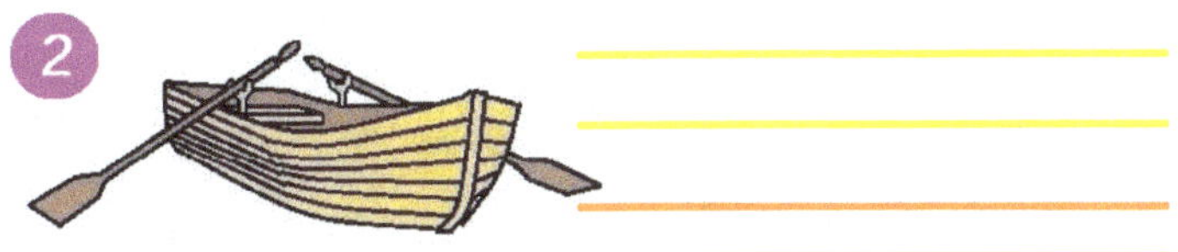

3

4

Listen and read along

New sight words: met   later   move   took

Deb liked t**oy** b**oa**ts.

Deb met a bad b**oy**.

Later, Deb met the b**oy** AGAIN!

Deb was angry!

Deb took the b**oy**'s c**oa**t and b**oa**t!

UNIT 3 Vowel Combinations

Listen, point, and make the sound:   Words with ou, ow, ar, or

Tracks 20-29

Track 25

1 **ou ow**

2 **ar** 3 **or**

Listen, point, and say the word: 

Track 26

1 h + **ou**se = h**ou**se  house

2 c + **ar** = c**ar**  car

3 h + **orn** = h**orn**  horn

Write the words

1 c + ow = __________ 

2 ou + t = __________ 

3 sh + ort = __________ 

4 sh + ark = __________ 

New Words

Listen, point and repeat the new words

Track 27

ou

house　　　out　　　shout

ow

brown　　　cow　　　owl

ar

car　　　fart　　　shark

or

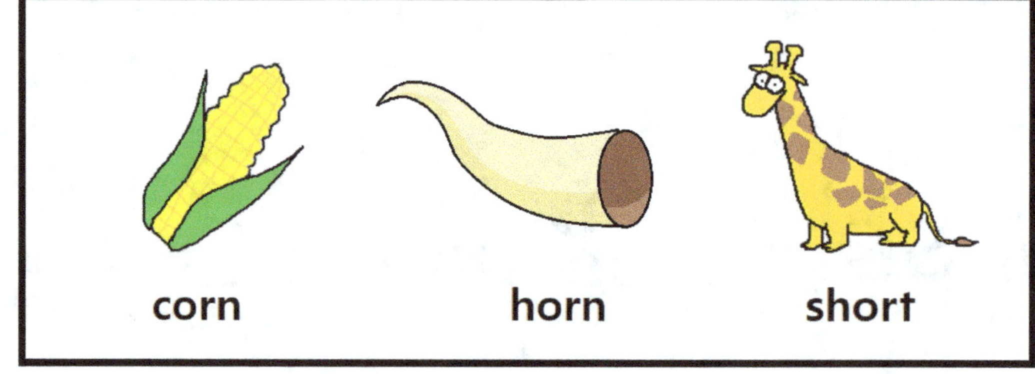

corn　　　horn　　　short

Exercises

Listen and complete the word

Track **28**

Tracks 20-29

1  c _ n    **2** h _ se

3 _ _ t   **4** _ _ l 

5 br _ n   **6** f _ t 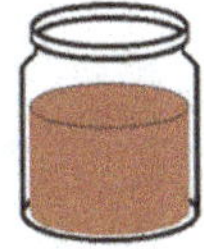

Listen and circle the right letters AND picture

Track **29**

1 ou ow ar or    **2** ou ow ar or 

3 ou ow ar or    **4** ou ow ar or 

5 ou ow ar or 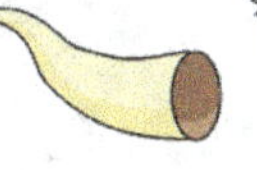   **6** ou ow ar or 

Exercises

Circle the word you hear

Tracks 30-39

Track 30

  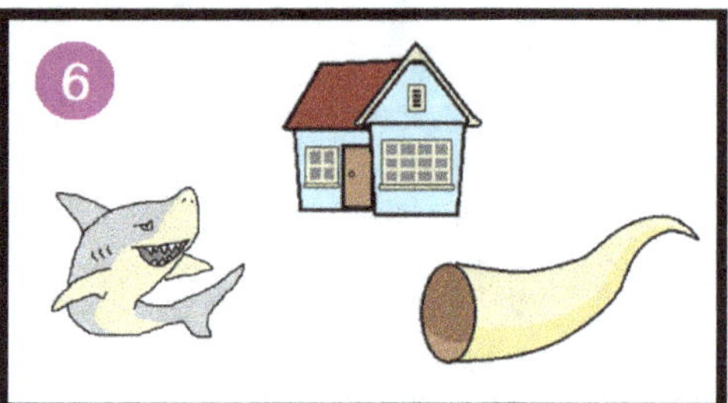

Circle the vowel sound you hear

Track 31

1. ou ow ar or   2. ou ow ar or

3. ou ow ar or   4. ou ow ar or

Chant

Track 32

Brown cows eating corn

In a house

Did you fart?

Did you fart?

Get out of the house!

Write the word to match the picture

Tracks 30-39

1  

2 

3  

4 

Listen and read along

Track 33

New sight words: okay

Review

Listen, point, and repeat all the words

Track
34

Tracks 30-39

1 ai / ay

| sail | train | wait |
| day | play | say |

2 ee / ea

| feet | teeth | tree |
| eat | meat | teach |

3 oa / ow

| boat | coat | soap |
| bowl | slow | throw |

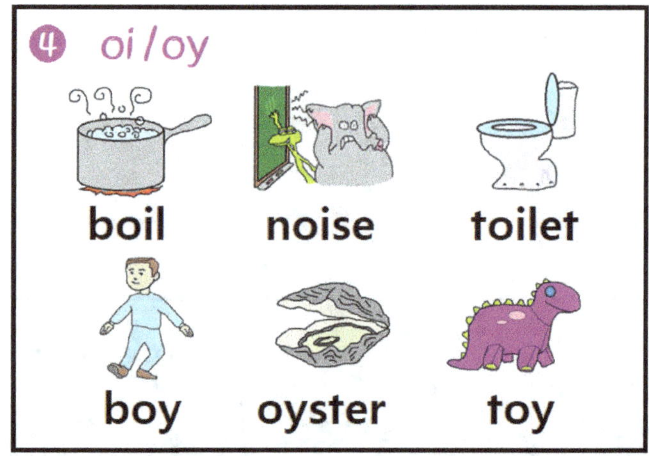

4 oi / oy

| boil | noise | toilet |
| boy | oyster | toy |

5 ou / ow

| house | out | shout |
| brown | cow | owl |

6 ar / or

| car | fart | shark |
| corn | horn | short |

Review

Say the word and write it

1 

2 

3 

4 

5 

Now put the numbers in the boxes according to sound

oy	ee	ay	ou	oa

More Sounds

Long and Short Sounds

Tracks 30-39

When two vowels come together they might
make a long vowel sound...

Track
35

...or they might make a SHORT one!

Track
36

Track
37

We don't know what they will do.

Cool R

People say R is bossy, but we think maybe the vowels think
it's so cool they just let it make all the noise.

Tracks 30-39

Together they often sound like this:

Track
38

UNIT 4   Vowel Combinations

Listen, point, and make the sound: **Track 39** Words with oo, oo, ew, ue

Tracks 30-39

1

oo
SHORT

2

oo ew ue

Listen, point, and say the word: **Track 40**

1 c + ook = cook  cook

2 f + ood = food  food

3 ch + ew = chew  chew

Follow the rules

Write the words

1   **bl** + **ue** = _______________ 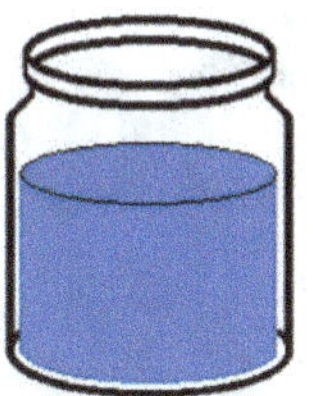

2   **f** + **oot** = _______________ 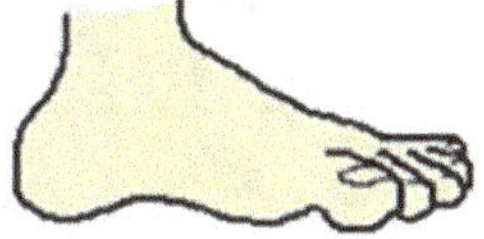
SHORT

3   **z** + **oo** = _______________ 

4   **n** + **ew** = _______________ 

New Words

Listen, point and repeat the new words

oo
(short)

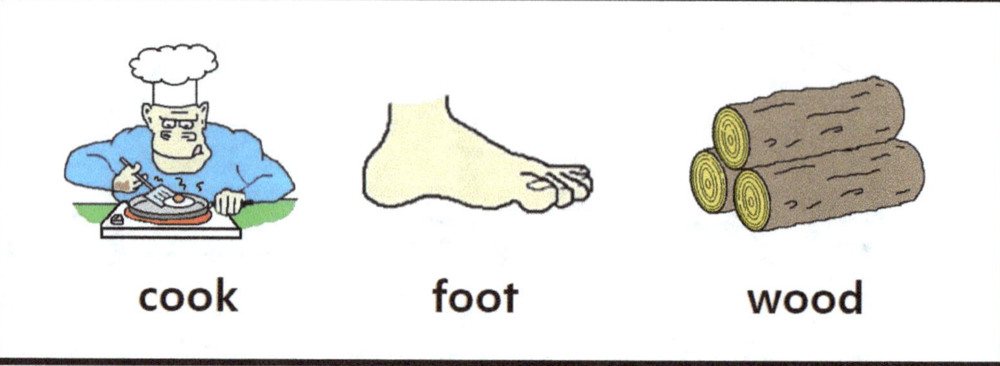

cook   foot   wood

oo

food   pool   zoo

ew

chew   new   stew

ue

blue   clue   glue

Exercises

Listen and complete the word

Tracks 40-49

1  w ___ d

2  p ___ l

3  c l ___

4  ___ st

5 ___ g l ___

6 f ___ d

Listen and circle the right letters AND picture

1 oo oo ew ue  
SHORT

2 oo oo ew ue  
SHORT

3 oo oo ew ue 
SHORT

4 oo oo ew ue 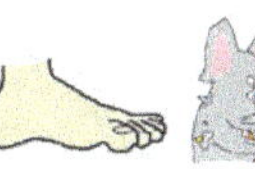
SHORT

5 oo oo ew ue  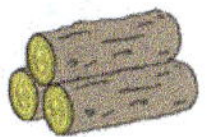
SHORT

6 oo oo ew ue  
SHORT

Exercises

Circle the word you hear

Track 44

Tracks 40-49

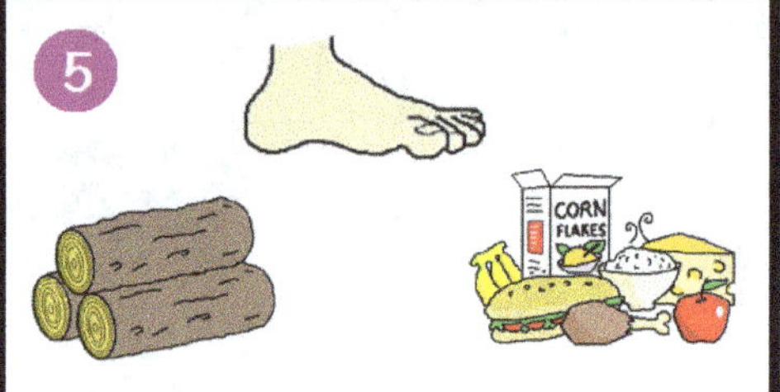
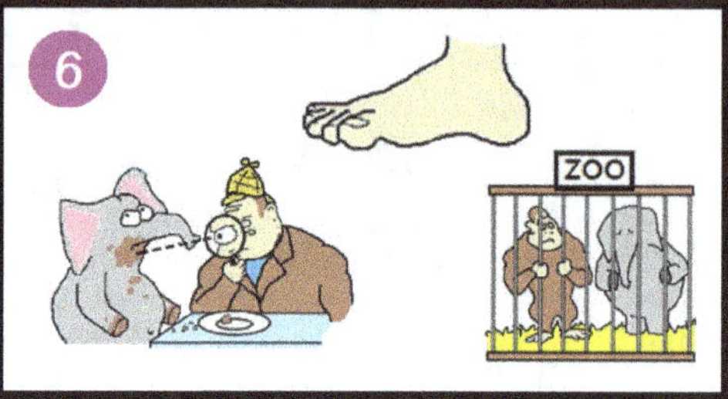

Circle the vowel sound you hear

Track 45

1. oo (SHORT) oo ew ue   2. oo (SHORT) oo ew ue

3. oo (SHORT) oo ew ue   4. oo (SHORT) oo ew ue

Chant

Track 46

New sight words: cannot

Don't put your foot in my food

Your foot I cannot chew

Don't put blue glue in my stew

I cannot chew blue glue

Write the word to match the picture

Tracks 40-49

 1 

2 

3 

4 

Listen and read along

Track 47

New sight words: our   cool

Listen, point, and make the sound:   Track 48   Words with er, ir, or, ur

Tracks 40-49

1

er   ir

or   ur

Listen, point, and say the word: Track 49

1   p + erm = perm  perm

2   g + irl = girl  girl

3   b + urp = burp  burp

Follow the rules

Write the words

1 w + ork = _________ 

2 teach + er = _________ 

3 d + irt = _________ 

4 f + ur = _________ 

New Words

Listen, point and repeat the new words

Track
50

er

germ | perm | teacher

ir

dirt | girl | stir

or

doctor | work | worm

ur

burp | fur | turn

Exercises

Listen and complete the word

Tracks 50-59

1  st

2 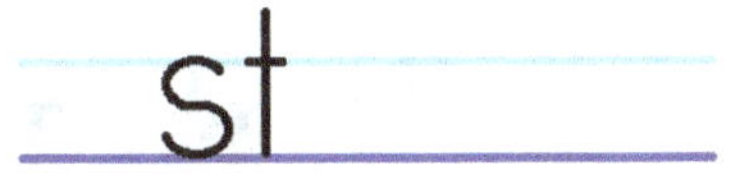 t n

3  doct

4 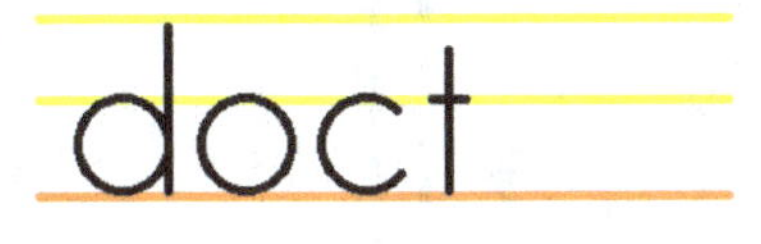 p m

5  d t

6  g m

Listen and circle the right letters AND picture

1 er ir ur or 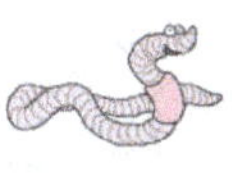 

2 er ir ur or 

3 er ir ur or 

4 er ir ur or 

5 er ir ur or  

6 er ir ur or  

Exercises

Circle the word you hear

Tracks 50-59

Circle the vowel sound you hear

1 er ir ur or   2 er ir ur or

3 er ir ur or   4 er ir ur or

Chant

Dirt and germs in my fur

My fur has dirt and germs

Dirt and worms in my perm

My perm has dirt and worms

Write the word to match the picture

Tracks 50-59

1 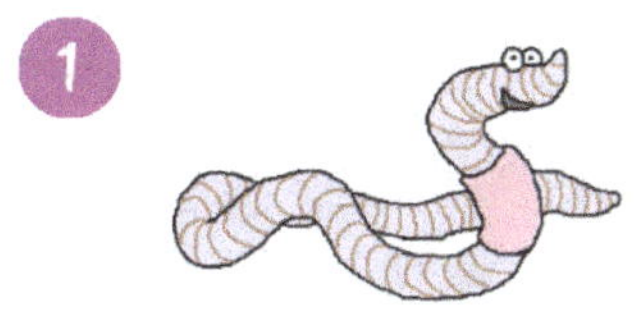

2 

3 

4 

Listen and read along

Track 56

Review

Say the word and write it

1 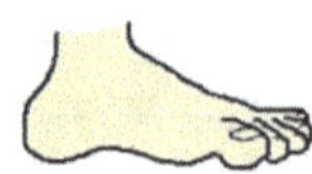 foot

2  germ

3  food

4  clue

5  chew

6  girl

Now put the numbers in the boxes according to sound

<table>
<tr><td>oo
SHORT</td><td>oo ew
ue</td><td>ir er</td></tr>
</table>

Review

1 

2 

3 

4 

5 

6 

Review

Listen, point, and repeat all the words

Tracks 50-59

Track
57

1 ai / ay

sail train wait

day play say

2 ee / ea

feet teeth tree

eat meat teach

3 oa / ow

boat coat soap

bowl slow throw

4 oi / oy

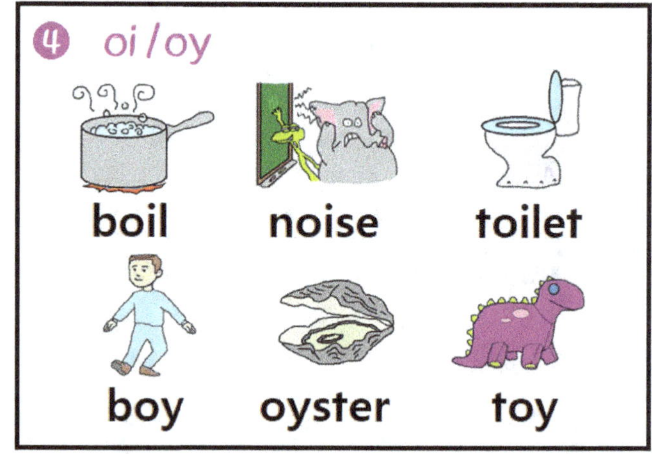

boil noise toilet

boy oyster toy

5 ou / ow

house out shout

brown cow owl

6 ar / or

car fart shark

corn horn short

Review

Track 58

Tracks 50-59

1 oo/oo

2 ew/ue

3 er/ir

4 or/ur

That's all there is!

Test

Listen and circle the word you hear

a | Track 59 b | Track 60 c | Track 61

1    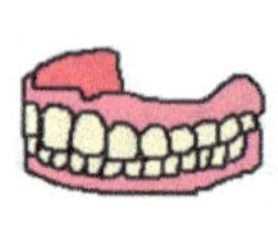  

2      

3      

4      

5      

Test

Listen and write ANY digraph that matches a | Track 62 b | Track 63 c | Track 64

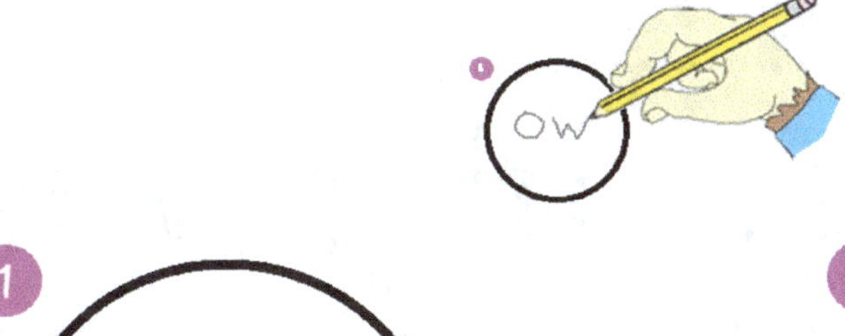

Tracks 60-68

1 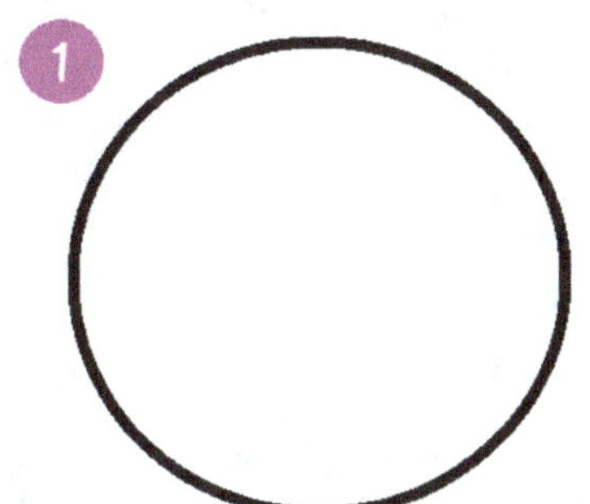

2 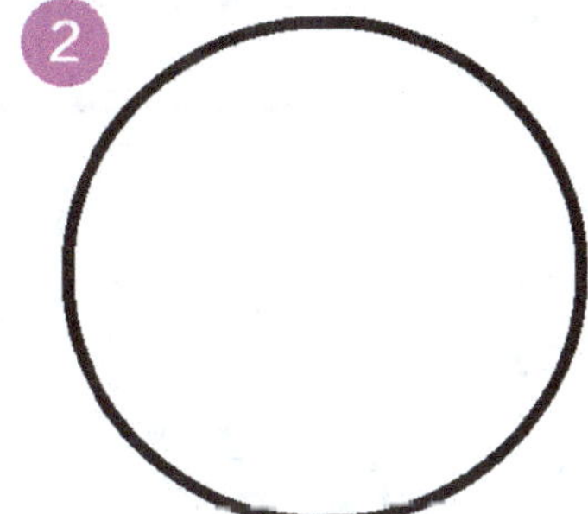

3 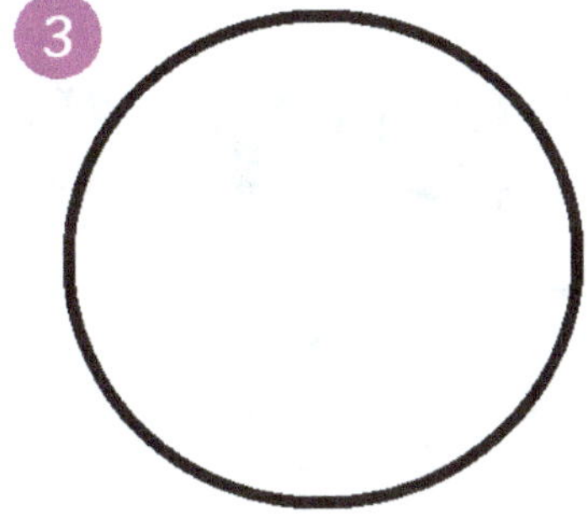

4 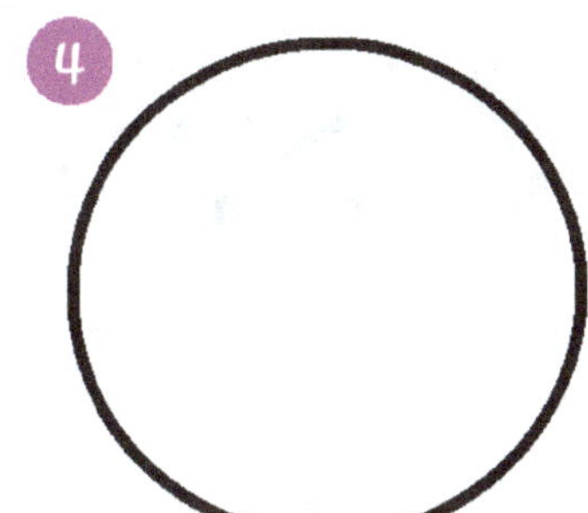

5 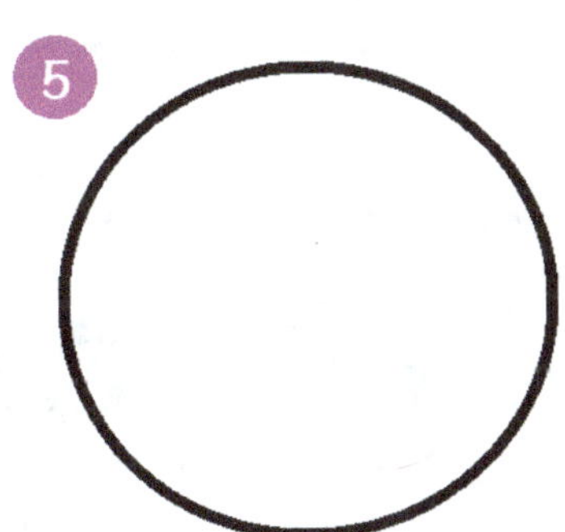

6 

Test

 Listen and circle the right combination a | Track 65 | b | Track 66 | c | Track 67

Tracks 60-68

1  ou ee ai ew oy

2  ew ou oa ea ir

3  oy oo ay ow or

4  er ow ea oo ar

5  ee ir ai oi oo

Test

Circle the right sound

Tracks 60-68

1  **ai** **oy**

2 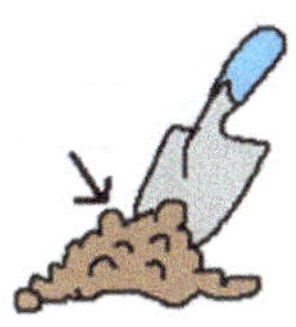 **ee** **ir**

3 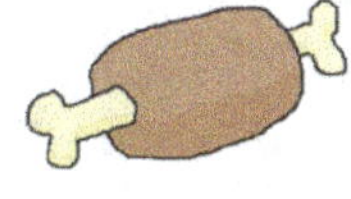 **ou** **ea**

4  **oo** **oa**

5  **ai** **ow**

6  **oa** **oi**

This is the end of the series!

Miller Gorilla

Eloise Elephant

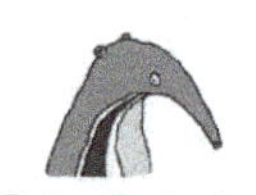

Isard Lizard

Noel Mole

Ludvig Pig

Sylvester fly

Debora Zebra

Reinhold Rhino

Eva Retriever

Peter Anteater

Steven Beaver

Luca Beluga

Matthew Hitch

Sunok Moon

Word List

Unit 1

sail	train	wait	day
play	say	feet	teeth
tree	eat	meat	teach

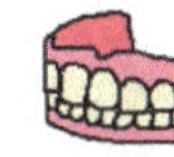

Unit 2

boat	coat	soap	bowl
slow	throw	boil	noise
toilet	boy	oyster	toy

  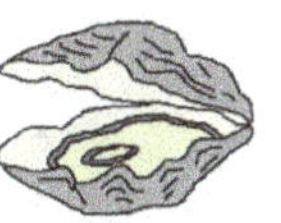 

Unit 3

house	out	shout	brown
cow	owl	car	fart
shark	corn	horn	short

 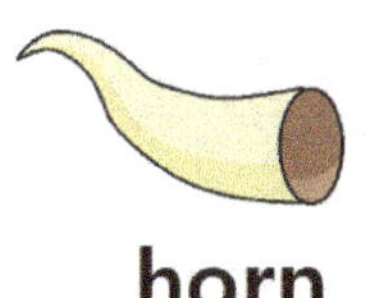

Word List

Unit 4

cook

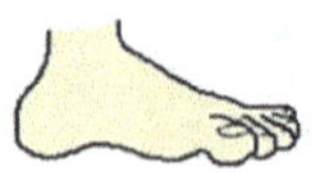
foot

wood

food

pool

zoo

chew

new

stew

blue

clue

glue

Unit 5

germ

perm

teacher

dirt

girl

stir

doctor

work

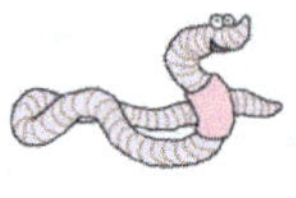
worm

burp

fur

turn

OUR SIGHT WORD FLASH CARDS!

with	way
please	or
them	met

OUR SIGHT WORD FLASH CARDS! 

later

move

took

okay

cannot

our

OUR SIGHT WORD FLASH CARDS!

cool

look

onto

are

too

we

OUR SIGHT WORD FLASH CARDS!

ready

again

check

can

wow

take

OUR SIGHT WORD FLASH CARDS!

his

as

here

sleep

don't

play

OUR SIGHT WORD FLASH CARDS! 

at

but

after

fly

for

best

OUR SIGHT WORD FLASH CARDS!

make

him

people

yell

my

am

OUR SIGHT WORD FLASH CARDS!

she	wear
so	will
want	give

OUR SIGHT WORD FLASH CARDS!

me

have

he

handsome

pretty

let's

OUR SIGHT WORD FLASH CARDS!

what

cent

see

call

must

need

OUR SIGHT WORD FLASH CARDS!

a / an

and

all

on

in

the

OUR SIGHT WORD FLASH CARDS!

not

lift

like

get

did

you

OUR SIGHT WORD FLASH CARDS! 

your

has

put

one

by

say

OUR SIGHT WORD FLASH CARDS!

go

to

win

had

it

wait

Phonics Series

Preschool:

Kindergarten:

Elementary School Junior:

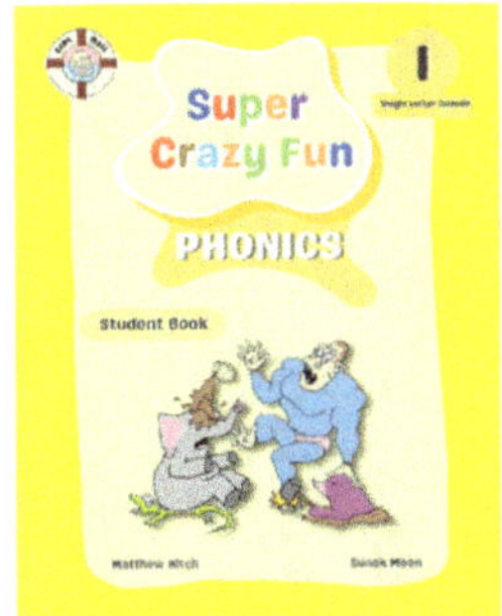
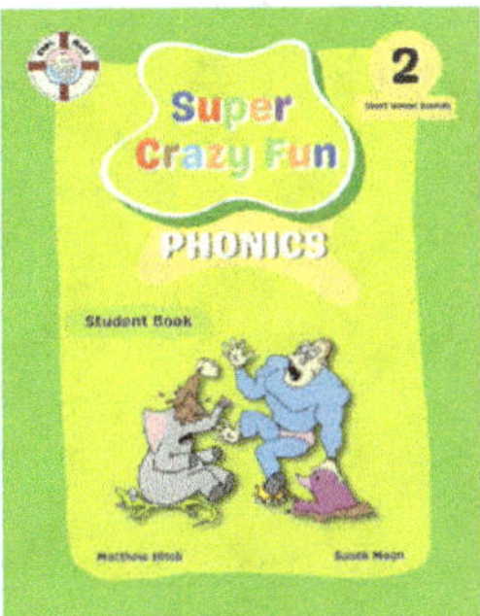

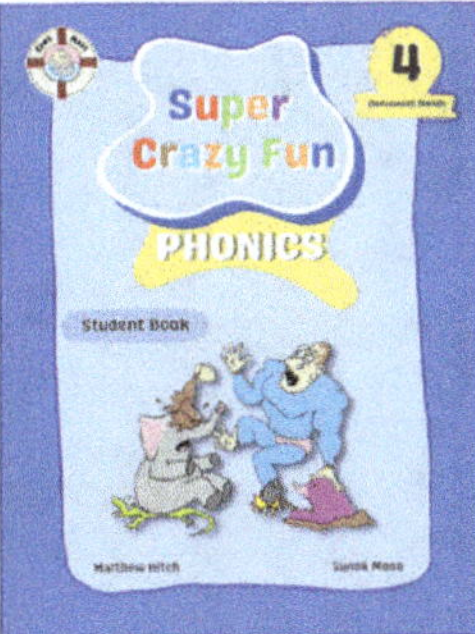

Elementary School Senior/Remedial: